THE GREAT BLACK MIGRATION

Bound for the

Promised Land

Also by Michael L. Cooper

From Slave to Civil War Hero: The Life and
Times of Robert Smalls

Playing America's Game: The Story of
Negro League Baseball

THE GREAT BLACK MIGRATION

Bound for the
Promised Land

Michael L. Cooper

Lodestar Books

DUTTON   NEW YORK

to Sharon and Tom, who stayed home

Library of Congress Cataloging-in-Publication Data

Cooper, Michael L.
   Bound for the promised land: the great black migration / Michael L. Cooper—1st ed.
      p.   cm.
   Includes bibliographical references and index.
   ISBN 0-525-67476-4 (alk. paper)
   1. Afro-Americans—Migrations—History—20th century—Juvenile literature. 2. Rural-urban migration—United States—History—20th century—Juvenile literature.   I. Title.
E185.6.C78   1995
973'.0496073—dc20   95-2611

Published in the United States by Lodestar Books,
an affiliate of Dutton Children's Books,
a division of Penguin Books USA Inc.,
375 Hudson Street, New York, New York 10014

Published simultaneously in Canada by McClelland & Stewart, Toronto

Editor: Virginia Buckley   Designer: Marilyn Granald

Printed in the U.S.A.   First Edition   10 9 8 7 6 5 4 3 2 1

Frontispiece photo: *Migrants waiting for a northbound train crowd a "colored only" waiting room in a Florida station.*
Florida State Archives

Contents

Acknowledgments

The staff in the photographs and prints division of the Schomburg Center for Research in Black Culture of the New York Public Library have been very helpful. Special thanks to Mary F. Yearwood, James Huffman, Anthony Toussaint, Linden Anderson, and Oneida Mitchell.

The Great Migration

As the Illinois Central Train rumbled across the Ohio River on the long railroad trestle from Kentucky to Evansville, Indiana, there were shouts of joy in the "colored only" passenger car. Dozens of people knelt in the aisle to pray. Then they sang a familiar church song of deliverance: "I done come out the land of Egypt, ain't that good news. O Canaan, sweet Canaan, I am bound for the land of Canaan."

For these African Americans, the South was Egypt, the land of bondage, and the North—on the other side of the Ohio River—was the promised land of Canaan. To them, the river symbolized the division between oppression and freedom, between despair and hope. The people on the train were part of an exodus that began in 1915 and continued until 1930. It is called the Great Migration.

Ever since the end of the Civil War, black people had been moving away from the South. At first, like other Americans and European immigrants, blacks went West. In the 1870s and 1880s, more than a hundred thousand former slaves settled on homesteads in Kansas and Oklahoma.

The following decade, there began a noticeable movement of blacks to the North, to such cities as Washington, D.C., Chicago, Philadelphia, and New York. This group of ambitious men and women was fleeing a southern caste system that confined blacks to menial jobs as servants and field hands. Black intellectual W. E. B. Du Bois called this movement the migration of the Talented Tenth. The nineteenth-century migrations to the West and North were small compared to the number of African Americans who caught "northern fever" in 1915.

The immediate cause of the Great Migration was World War I, which had begun a year earlier. Until then, it was the largest conflict in the history of the world. The Central Powers—Germany, the Austro-Hungarian Empire, and Italy—were fighting the Allies—France, Russia, and Great Britain. America entered the war against the Central Powers in 1917.

In the decades prior to the war, several million Russians, Italians, Irish, and Germans had immigrated to America. They were drawn by the abundance of jobs in the young nation's growing cities and industries. But the fighting, which involved most of the countries of Europe, abruptly curtailed the trans-Atlantic migration.

Suddenly, there were not enough workers in northern factories. At the same time, the war greatly increased demand for such manufactured goods as uniforms, canned foods, and steel, which was used in ships and tanks. The small number of black people who lived in northern cities usually worked as household servants or in service jobs as barbers or caterers. Few worked in industry, but the shortage of white laborers swung open the factory doors for African Americans.

Plentiful jobs at high wages caused a stampede to the industrial cities. Northern companies ran advertisements in southern newspapers and sent recruiters to find workers for factories, shipyards, steel mills, and railroads. In one day, three thousand young men in Jacksonville, Florida, climbed aboard a freight train that carried them to Pennsylvania to work on yard crews

In the South's plantation country, there were many similarities to "slavery time." Vagrancy laws in several states allowed sheriffs to force unemployed blacks to work. These laws were especially popular when there were shortages of field hands during the fall harvest. If the person refused the job, he was put in jail. "Judge gave me six months 'cause I wouldn't go to work," lamented a line from the song "Chain Gang Blues."

Another law prevented sharecroppers from quitting their jobs before the cotton had been picked. And yet another one permitted plantation owners to sell their field hands' debts. Since sharecroppers were legally obligated to work for the person to whom they owed money, selling their debts was like selling the people.

Planters could whip their field hands, just as in the days of slavery. "Most of the planters when they catch one of their hands stealing will take them out and give them a beating and that's the end of it," a white justice of the peace remarked matter-of-factly.

African Americans had few job choices. Women became maids, cooks, laundresses, or wet nurses. Men worked as field hands or as laborers at turpentine and saw mills. The cities offered black men a wide variety of jobs. In New Orleans, Louisiana, Charleston, South Carolina, and other coastal cities, black longshoremen loaded and unloaded cargo ships. They worked in steel mills in Birmingham, Alabama, and in tobacco warehouses in Richmond, Virginia.

There were unwritten and frequently changing codes about which jobs blacks could hold. At the turn of the century, whites forced black bricklayers and carpenters out of their trades. Richard Wright worked for an optician who promised to teach the young man the craft of making lenses. But white lens makers, resentful that a black might join their ranks, harassed Wright until he quit his job.

A boy plowing
Library of Congress

In the South it was a serious breach of custom to treat whites and blacks equally. Whites always had to be deferred to regardless of how skilled a black worker was or how long he had been doing a particular job. "If a thousand whites work at a place," one man complained, "each one there is my 'boss.'"

Because white people never expected African Americans to be anything other than laborers and servants, they did not think black children needed education. "The Negro isn't permitted to advance and their education is money thrown away," explained Mississippi's U.S. Senator James K. Vardaman. Southern schools had been legally segregated since the U.S. Supreme Court, in the 1896 landmark case *Plessy versus*

Ferguson, allowed separate but equal public services for black and white people. The court conveniently ignored the real issue—that for black people, such services as schools, libraries and hospitals rarely existed.

In 1910, two of the South's largest cities, Montgomery and Atlanta, had no high schools for African American teenagers although both cities had large black populations. There were only six public high schools in all of Mississippi, Alabama, Georgia, and Louisiana, and only two of these offered four-year programs. In those same states, fewer than half of the black children under age ten attended school.

Black teachers were dedicated, but few had more than an eighth-grade education. "If a man could write, count to a hundred and spell Constantinople," an African American commented, "he was competent enough to teach at a Negro school in the rural districts of Mississippi." These teachers also were poorly paid. In one typical South Carolina county, white teachers earned three hundred and forty dollars a year while black teachers earned eighty-four dollars a year.

The existing public schools were frequently housed in share-croppers' cabins, stores, or churches. Some of these buildings, a teacher said, were in such disrepair that "when it rained, the water not only came through the top but through the sides as well."

In small towns and in the countryside, spring planting and fall harvesting kept school terms short. "Soon as our school closed down, cotton would be ready to chop. We little colored children had to jump in the white man's field and work for what we could get," one man remembered.

Although black people's taxes helped support white public schools, tax money was not spent on black schools. It was no secret why this was so. "The white people want to keep the

Negro in his place," a professor at the University of Mississippi commented, "and educated people have a way of making their own places and their own terms."

Some blacks were educated and did own land, houses, and businesses, but an unwritten rule, the "Dixie limit," kept them from becoming too prosperous. "If we own a good farm or horse, or cow, or bird dog, or yoke of oxen," one black Southerner explained, "we are harassed until we are bound to sell, give away or run away, before we can have any peace in our lives."

Because the police and courts did not treat the two races equally, African Americans in the South had little protection. A prominent lawyer and planter expressed a common belief: "Murder, thieving, lying, violence—I sometimes suspect the Negro doesn't regard these as crimes or sins, or even as regrettable occurrences. He commits them casually with no apparent feeling of guilt."

White police and judges often ignored or regarded lightly crimes, even murder, by blacks against blacks. But blacks who committed crimes against whites, no matter how minor, could be brutally treated.

In Mississippi in 1911, a white farmer killed two unarmed black men for trespassing. The sheriff did not charge the farmer with murder or with any crime. A few years later, in another part of the state, a mob burst into a courtroom and seized a black man accused of poisoning a well. The mob lynched the man and, later that day, lynched his wife and her mother.

A few years later in southern Georgia, near the town of Valdosta, a white mob went on a rampage after a planter had been murdered. They lynched several African Americans, including a pregnant woman, who was doused with gasoline and set afire. After forcing a man to confess to the planter's murder, the mob shot and castrated him, then dragged his body through the streets of Valdosta.

Even the few educated and relatively prosperous blacks were not safe. Soon after America entered World War I in 1917, Dr. J. A. Miller, a black physician in Vicksburg, Mississippi, was assaulted for not buying enough war bonds. He was tarred and feathered by a crowd that included a policeman, paraded along Main Street, and put in jail. City officials ordered the physician to sell his home and leave town if he wished to remain alive.

Southern blacks had few choices other than to live with Jim Crow laws, cheating planters, and murderous mobs. They had only one way to protest: They could move.

Chapter 2

Bound for the Promised Land

> With ever watchful eyes and bearing scars, visible and invisible, I headed North, full of a hazy notion that life could be lived with dignity.
> —Richard Wright, *Black Boy*

In 1916, the black-owned *Chicago Defender* and other newspapers began reporting on the growing number of African Americans hastily leaving the South. One article from a town in the plantation country of eastern Georgia stated, "There are so many leaving here that Waycross will be desolate soon."

An article in a Macon, Georgia, paper complained, "Everybody seems to be asleep about what is going on right under our noses—that is, everybody but those farmers who waked [*sic*] up one morning recently to find every Negro over twenty-one on their places gone—to Cleveland, to Pittsburgh, to Chicago, to Indianapolis. Better jobs, better treatment, higher pay—the bait being held out is swallowed by thousands of them about us."

Older migrants planned their trips to the North carefully, while younger ones often left abruptly. One man recalled the day he decided to go north: "I was plowing in the field and it was real hot. And I stayed with some of the boys who would leave home and [come] back . . . and would have money and have clothes. I didn't have that. We all grew up together. And

I said, 'Well, as long as I stay here I'm not goin' to get nowhere.' And I tied that mule to a tree and caught a train."

In letters and visits home, people who had already migrated encouraged others to do the same. "I go home every two years," said a man who had moved from St. Helena Island, South Carolina, to New York City's Harlem. "Everybody on the island nearly knows me. When I go home my mother's house can't hold all the people. I have set up all night talking to the people down there about the things I've seen up here. Then when I finish one or two of them will say, 'Uncle Joe, can't you take me back up there with you?'"

The Great Migration drew not only young men and women escaping the monotony of rural life but also older people, who left their jobs and homes hoping to find a better life up North for their families.

Robert Horton, a man in his mid-thirties, was a barber in Hattiesburg, Mississippi. He owned his shop and he was a deacon in his church. Horton's barbershop was a popular place on Saturdays for men to have their hair cut or just to gather and exchange news and gossip.

These men frequently talked about local people who had moved. Horton's older brother already had left Hattiesburg for Chicago. When he came home for visits, he was dressed in fashionable clothes and spent money freely. Horton described his brother's life in Chicago, and the other men had stories of their own about high wages, schools, voting, big-league baseball, night clubs, and pretty women.

By the fall of 1916, Horton and his friends had decided they would move to Chicago. Forty men and women formed a migration club. Such clubs were common among the migrants. By banding together, they could share information about housing, schools, and jobs. Also, the railroads gave fare discounts to groups traveling together. And the club members provided a ready network of supportive friends in the strange new city.

Horton and his club moved to the South Side of Chicago. Many of the city's black people lived in this neighborhood of run-down one- and two-story frame houses squeezed between the stockyards to the west and the white community of Hyde Park on the shore of Lake Michigan to the east.

It was a good neighborhood for Horton's business. He opened the Hattiesburg Shaving Shop, which became a gathering place for Mississippi migrants. Soon the barber began receiving letters from old friends and neighbors asking about the availability of jobs and the cost of apartments.

The *Chicago Defender* was another important source of information about life and opportunities in the North. During the early years of the Great Migration, the *Defender* became the nation's largest black-owned newspaper and the single most important advocate of migration. Its publisher, Robert Abbott, had grown up near Savannah, Georgia. He moved to Chicago in the 1890s, went to law school, and in 1905 founded the weekly newspaper.

By 1916, the *Defender* had a circulation of 33,000. The next year circulation nearly tripled, and by 1919, some 130,000 copies were being sold across the nation. The weekly paper was delivered to 1,500 southern towns and cities from Savannah to Houston, Texas. An observer said that copies were "passed house to house in Negro communities to the point of being worn out." In a letter to the newspaper, one enthusiastic reader wrote, "I have had the pleasure of reading the *Defender* for the first time in my life and I never dreamed that there was such a race paper published and I must say that it's some paper."

The *Defender* earnestly began promoting migration by declaring May 15, 1917, as the date for the "Great Northern

*Robert S. Abbott, the founder of
the influential* Chicago Defender
Schomburg Center for Research in
Black Culture

Drive." On that   day, Abbott's paper predicted, African Americans by the tens of thousands would leave the South.

The newspaper also encouraged the exodus by describing Chicago as a place where black people could enjoy rights, opportunities, and pleasures denied them in the South. There were articles about Rube Foster and his all-black professional baseball team, the American Giants, and on heavyweight boxer Jack Johnson's victories and the black champion's big cars and white girlfriends. Stories about interracial romance could only be discussed in whispers because it was the biggest taboo in the South. There, black men faced almost certain death for even casting an admiring glance at a white woman.

Readers especially marveled over feature articles on Wendell Phillips High School. This large Chicago school offered its students science labs, literary clubs, and debating societies. It also had baseball, football, and basketball teams. Even more surprising to Southerners, whites as well as blacks attended Wendell Phillips.

Another appealing feature of Chicago life was Provident Hospital. Because of poverty, segregation, and the scarcity of black physicians, most southern blacks were born, grew old, and died without ever visiting a doctor. But Provident Hospital on South Dearborn Street had been founded by African Americans. Its chief administrator was a black surgeon. The hospital trained black nurses and physicians and served patients of both races.

Articles in the *Defender* and letters and visits from friends and relatives all created the impression that the North was practically paradise. One man said he had "never been in the North no further than Texas," but he had heard "how much better the colored people are treated up there than they are down here." The land above the Mason-Dixon line assumed a mythical quality expressed by songs and poems with such wishful titles as "Bound for the Promised Land" and "Land of Hope."

More people would have migrated if poverty had not held them back. The *Defender* and churches constantly received requests for financial help. A ticket from New Orleans to Chicago cost about twenty dollars, which was a lot of money for poor Southerners. One man wrote to a church requesting not only train fare but also "a suitcase to put things in."

The Great Migration puzzled, alarmed, and angered white Southerners. Blacks "contaminated with northern social and political dreams of equality need not return," thundered Mississippi's Governor Theodore Bilbo. "We have all the room in the world for what we know as N-i-g-g-e-r-s, but none whatsoever for colored ladies and gentlemen."

Southerners suddenly realized how much they depended on black workers. "It would be quite as inconvenient for Mississippi to do without Negro labor as it would to do without mules," commented one newspaper. The migration caused much complaining among white people who lost their best field hands and maids.

Some people forcibly tried to stop the exodus. In Savannah, police arrested two hundred African Americans waiting for a northbound train. Many railroad stations would not accept tickets purchased in the North and mailed to relatives and friends in the South. In one small Mississippi town, local officials closed the station and refused to let trains make scheduled stops.

White Southerners especially hated black newspapers and magazines. One paper called the *Defender* "the greatest disturbing element that has yet entered Georgia." They beat or jailed people for selling or even reading black publications from the North. In Georgia, a boy selling the *Defender* was murdered. And in Mississippi, a court fined a minister four hundred dollars and sentenced him to five months in jail for selling *Crisis,* the magazine of the National Association for the Advancement of Colored People (NAACP). Many of the hundred thousand African Americans who worked on trains as porters, maids, cooks, and dining-car waiters quietly distributed the *Defender* as they traveled among southern cities and towns.

Whites looked for scapegoats to blame for the migration. "The Negroes who have gone North haven't gone because of any bad treatment accorded them here," said a Nashville paper, expressing a common belief. "They have gone because agents came South in search of labor and offered them higher wages than they were making here."

Northerners did go South to recruit black Southerners,

particularly in the early years of the war, when there was an enormous need for men in the steel mills, in the meat-packing houses, and on the railroads. But the influence of labor agents was limited because white politicians passed laws making their work nearly impossible.

City officials in Macon, Georgia, discouraged agents by requiring a license fee of twenty-five thousand dollars, and personal recommendations from ten local ministers, ten manufacturers, and twenty-five business people. In Mississippi, labor agents could be fined five hundred dollars and imprisoned. Eventually, as news of plentiful jobs at high wages caused tens of thousands of workers to flood the North, agents were no longer needed.

White Southerners were not the only ones who opposed the exodus; some African American leaders were against it too. "[I have] never seen any part of the world where it seemed to me the masses of the Negro people would be better off than right here in these southern states," declared Booker T. Washington. Black businessmen and preachers discouraged people from leaving because their jobs depended on the black population. "The great exodus of the colored people from the South has caused my work to lapse until I am unable to get a living out of it," complained an insurance agent in Selma, Alabama. Many preachers and businessmen followed their congregations and customers.

Other black leaders, especially those living in the North, encouraged the mass movement. Abbott's *Defender* said the Great Migration would lead to a "newer and more significant emancipation."

Chapter 3

The Black Metropolis

> I should have been here twenty years ago. I just begin to feel like a man. My children are going to the same school with the whites and I don't have to humble to no one. I have registered. Will vote in the next election.
>
> —A migrant's letter to southern friends

So many migrants were arriving daily at Chicago's Illinois Central railroad station in the spring of 1917 that the Travelers Aid Society hired its first "colored assistant." Travelers Aid needed a black assistant because southern African Americans were afraid to ask white people for directions. The Southerners' fears diminished as they saw signs of the racial equality they had heard about.

"I just held my breath, for I thought any minute they would start something," a woman recalled the first time she saw whites and blacks sitting side by side on a streetcar. "Then I saw nobody noticed it, and I just thought this is a real place for Negroes."

Despite the black assistant at Travelers Aid, newly arrived migrants preferred asking the station's black porters which streetcars would carry them to the city's Negro district. Every northern city had one. There was Harlem in New York, the Hill in Pittsburgh, and Paradise Valley in Detroit. In the first years of the exodus, tens of thousands of newcomers doubled and tripled the populations of these neighborhoods.

"South State Street was in its glory then," recalled Langston Hughes, who became a prominent writer during the 1920s. He described the South Side's main street as "a teeming Negro street with crowded theatres, restaurants, and cabarets. And excitement from noon to noon. Midnight was like day. The street was full of workers and gamblers, prostitutes and pimps, church folks and sinners."

Newcomers moved there to be near friends and relatives. They also enjoyed being surrounded by the familiar sights, sounds, and smells of the South. There were fraternal orders, churches, beauty parlors, and barbershops. Restaurants served familiar southern food such as corn bread, collards, sweet potatoes, chitterlings, pig snouts, and black-eyed peas.

The hostility of whites prevented African Americans from moving to other sections of the city. "Niggers are undesirable neighbors and entirely irresponsible and vicious," declared one organization of white homeowners. Discrimination in northern states was against the law; nonetheless it existed, and open racism increased as more and more Southerners moved north.

Hughes remembered crossing the imaginary "dead line" separating Irish and black communities on Chicago's South Side. He "was set upon and beaten by a group of white boys, who said they didn't allow niggers in that neighborhood." And an Irish gang known as Ragan's Colts assaulted young African Americans who tried to play on the baseball diamonds in Washington Park. Even policemen stopped blacks from using the city parks.

In downtown Chicago, African Americans faced various kinds of discrimination. Buses, street cars, and trains were integrated, but restaurants, theaters, and department stores discouraged black patrons. Some restaurants refused service to all blacks. Others ignored them, served bad food, or overcharged. Theater ushers steered blacks to balcony seats, and department store clerks directed them to basements, where only poor-quality merchandise was sold.

In their coverage of the "Negro problem," Chicago's white-owned newspapers printed inflammatory headlines such as "NEGROES ARRIVE BY THE THOUSANDS—PERIL TO HEALTH." A *Chicago Tribune* article described migrants as having "a child-like helplessness in the matter of sanitation and housing," and "they have almost no standard of morals." In 1917, hostility between the growing black population and whites caused a race riot in East St. Louis, Illinois. Fifty people died. Afterward, the *Tribune* advised "BLACK MAN, STAY SOUTH."

Despite such warnings from people North and South, the exodus continued. Migrants moved to Chicago for jobs, and they were not disappointed. Steel mills hired thousands of black laborers between 1916 and 1918. Illinois Steel employed just 35 blacks in 1916, but two years later it employed 1,209 black workers. During those same years, the number of black employees at a large slaughterhouse jumped from 311 to 3,069.

Migrants found ready employment in the slaughterhouses, stockyards, and meat-packing plants. "During the war it was easy for blacks who didn't mind starting at the bottom to get a job," recalled a railroad porter. "A Negro could always get a job in the stockyards."

These jobs were simple but often unpleasant. In the slaughter-houses, as many as 150 workers participated in the assembly-line process of butchering a single animal. Each person had a specialized job, from herding live animals into a pen to carrying the dressed carcasses into a cooler. One worker did nothing but cut off the animals' heads, while another sawed off their legs. On the killing floor, men stood in sticky pools of water and warm blood. The frightened animals bellowed and shrieked

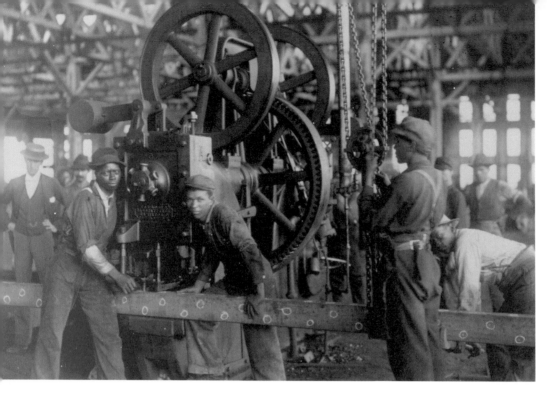

Black men in a steel mill
Library of Congress

Slaughterhouse workers prepare beef carcasses.
The Cincinnati Historical Society

continuously before they were killed by hard sledgehammer blows to their heads. Workers labored ten to twelve hours a day, six days a week, in rooms that were poorly lit and ventilated.

The wartime labor shortage opened many jobs for women. Slaughterhouses hired them to trim fat and cartilage from the hearts, kidneys, and tongues of cattle and hogs. They graded the cuts of pork and beef or prepared and canned meats. Other women tanned hides to make belts and shoes.

As menial and unpleasant as these jobs were, they represented progress to optimistic black leaders. "The most significant economic change among Negroes in the last ten or twenty years has been their influx into northern cities," observed Du Bois at the beginning of the Great Migration. An article in the *Defender* declared: "Our entrance into factories, workshops and every other industry open to man places us on an entirely different footing; we become a factor in the economy to be reckoned with. We are on trial."

That trial would decide a question: Were blacks actually capable of working in factories or, as whites argued, were they suited only to jobs as field hands and servants?

Factory work differed from farm work, so the Southerners had to learn new habits. Sharecroppers spent long days in the fields for a couple of weeks during spring planting and fall harvesting. But factory jobs required long workdays for months and years. This seemed unbearable to some workers.

"I just had to have some day of the week off for pleasure," one man explained. Frequently that day came after being paid on Friday. "Saturday is not a national holiday," a foreman scolded a group of migrants.

In time, perceptions of black abilities changed. "The Negro up here from the South never heard of working six days a week

A factory worker. Many jobs opened to women during the war.
Schomburg Center for Research in Black Culture

and being on time," one employer observed. "But with a little persistent effort and showing him that it is necessary, he soon learns the system the same as the others."

Chicago's community leaders felt obligated to instruct the new arrival in proper behavior on the job, on the street, and even at home. Abbott's *Defender* criticized the Southerners' manners and habits. "Keep your mouth shut, please! There is entirely too much loud talking on the streetcars among our

Hostile whites forced Ida B. Wells-Barnett to leave Memphis because of her newspaper articles denouncing lynching.
Schomburg Center for Research in Black Culture

newcomers." Or, "Go clean up North. In the South a premium was put on filth and uncleanliness. In the North a badge of honor is put on the man or woman who is clean." The migrants' lack of urban sophistication, Abbott believed, increased prejudice and discrimination against all black people.

The *Defender*'s publisher was not alone in his attempts to change the newcomers. He was joined by other black community leaders such as journalist Ida B. Wells-Barnett and real estate broker Jesse Binga. These prominent African Americans had been among the earlier group of migrants, whom Du Bois called the Talented Tenth. Unlike previous black business and community leaders, whose success depended on white patronage, the new generation of leaders looked to the growing black communities instead. They created charities and other organizations to help the newcomers adjust to city life.

One of the most important organizations was the National Urban League, which was founded in 1911. It had offices in every northern city by the end of the decade. The Chicago Urban League was founded in late 1915, and in its first two years helped more than twenty thousand people find jobs and homes. The league's mission, according to its first president, was to assist migrants in the transition from rural to urban life. The newcomers, who had few other places to go for assistance, filled the league's office in search of jobs and affordable places to live.

Reformers, both white and black, founded the league in the spirit of the times known as progressivism. Progressives believed in reason, truth, and enlightened democracy to bring about social change. Several black progressives created smaller organizations to help blacks in the city. Wells-Barnett founded the Negro Friendship League, which operated a lodging house, an employment agency, and a reading room. The Wabash YMCA, one of the most important black institutions in prewar Chicago, organized baseball teams and glee clubs among black workers in local factories.

Reformers believed young women were especially vulnerable to the evils of the city. Black women organized a branch of the YWCA in 1915 that offered vocational training, a library, and summer camps. Other organizations, such as Chicago's Club Home for Colored Girls and the Julia Johnson Home for Working Girls, were supervised residences offering single women inexpensive and safe places to live.

The most important institution was the church. Migrants

All-black YMCA chapters taught migrants new skills such as auto mechanics.
Schomburg Center for Research in Black Culture

more than doubled the membership of the city's largest black church, Mount Olivet Baptist Church, from four thousand in 1915 to nine thousand by 1920. During these years, Olivet moved into a larger building and was able to offer its members social clubs, sports teams, a kindergarten, and an employment bureau.

When the exodus began, Baptist and Methodist churches dominated black religious life in Chicago. The established churches were usually controlled by a group of people some-

31

As poor migrants crowded into Chicago's South Side, middle-class families started moving into white neighborhoods. These families, who often were City Hall employees or railroad porters, resented the coarse ways of the newcomers. A black man who had moved from the heart of the South Side complained that "the same class of Negroes who ran us away from Thirty-seventh Street are moving out there. They creep along slowly like a disease."

But blacks who moved into white neighborhoods frequently found worse problems than those they left behind.

Chapter 4

Red Summer

> Despite the possible justice of Negro demands, the fact is that the races are not living in harmony.
>
> —*Chicago Tribune,* July 29, 1919

In Chicago, as in other cities, the sudden arrival of tens of thousands of southern blacks alarmed white residents. Some of these frightened people responded violently.

In the first four years of the Great Migration, there were fifty-eight bombings in Chicago. The bombs were aimed at black families who had moved into white neighborhoods such as Kenwood, Hyde Park, and Grand Boulevard. The most frequent target was Jesse Binga. His real estate firm had sold houses in the white neighborhood where he lived to black families. Binga's home and office were bombed seven times.

The violence peaked soon after the war in Europe ended in late 1918. The armistice abruptly halted demand for war materials and caused a recession. The steel mills and slaughterhouses slowed production. Many workers, especially women and African Americans, lost their jobs. Blacks had been hired "solely on account of the shortage of labor," one company official admitted. "As soon as the situation clears itself no more colored help will be employed."

The summer of 1919 was so violent and so bloody that it has been called Red Summer. There were seventy-five lynchings

A mob chasing a black man, who was later stoned to death
Chicago Historical Society

and twenty-seven riots across the country that summer. The worst riot of all occurred in Chicago.

Racial violence had kept the city on tenterhooks for weeks. In late June, stepping up their attacks on African Americans, white gangs murdered two black men. A week later, a fight in a newly integrated neighborhood left one black man dead and six others injured.

Then, on a Sunday in late July, young Eugene Williams drowned in Lake Michigan. The teenager had been swimming at the public beach between Twenty-sixth and Twenty-ninth streets, the only city beach on the lake that African Americans were permitted to use. Black bathers accused whites of throwing rocks at the boy because he had swum near the white section. The police ignored the accusations, and angry blacks attacked several white people. That night, gangs of young men assaulted African Americans passing through in white neighborhoods.

The following morning was quiet, and everyone thought a major riot had been avoided. But that afternoon, whites attacked black workers leaving the stockyards. Men were pulled from streetcars and beaten. Blacks retaliated by attacking shopkeepers, truck drivers, and other whites on the South Side. After dark, cars full of white men drove up and down the streets of the South Side randomly shooting at people and houses. The national guard, helped by heavy rain, stopped the violence by the end of the week. Fifteen whites and twenty-

A couple being escorted to safety during the Chicago riot
Chicago Historical Society

year later, quickly grew to become the nation's largest black-owned insurance company. Its advertisements attracted customers by appealing to racial solidarity and pride.

The Binga State Bank, founded by Jesse Binga, received a state charter in 1919. The venture had special significance: "A Negro bank is more than an institution for financial savings and transactions," declared the National Urban League magazine *Opportunity.* "It is the symbol for the Negroes' aspirations to enter the commercial life of the nation."

Successful businesses, combined with the growing number of voters, gave blacks more power in politics. People who had been denied the ballot down South were eager to register up North. The city's politicians took notice of this fast-growing community of voters.

"Big Bill" Thompson eagerly sought black support in his 1915 campaign for mayor. He appealed to the all-black Appomattox Club, which had a membership that included the city's most successful men. Thompson promised black voters "the best opportunities you've ever had if you elect me."

After winning the election, the new mayor kept his word and appointed blacks to City Hall jobs. Thompson helped Oscar DePriest, a former house painter, work his way up through the ranks of the Republican party. In 1915, DePriest became Chicago's first black alderman. In 1928, the politician was elected to the United States Congress, the only African American in Congress at the time.

While DePriest was building his political career, other black leaders were busy creating organizations that were mirror images of the white organizations from which blacks were largely excluded. African Americans founded newspapers, banks, hospitals, and churches. They had their own political machines, self-help organizations, charities, and business groups. Sports also attracted the interest of entrepreneurs.

Customers at a black-owned bank
Schomburg Center for Research in Black Culture

Ever since the beginning of the century, major league baseball had barred black athletes. The game was America's most
popular sport, loved by blacks as well as whites. In February
1920, a group of businessmen met in a Kansas City, Missouri,
YMCA to organize the Negro National League. The NNL
consisted of eight midwestern teams, including two from
Chicago.

The man most responsible for creating the league was Rube
Foster. The Texas native had been a pitcher before becoming
owner and manager of the Chicago American Giants. By

organizing the NNL, Foster said he wanted to "create a profession that would equal the earning capacity of any other profession [and] keep colored baseball from the control of whites [and] do something concrete for the loyalty of the race." In 1924, the Negro National League in the Midwest and the Eastern Colored League, which included teams from New York, Philadelphia, and other northeastern cities, began the annual Negro World Series.

The key to self-reliance and success, many people believed, was education. By moving north, migrants gave themselves and their children a chance to go to good schools.

Adults took evening classes at Wendell Phillips High School. They paid one dollar for elementary classes and two dollars for high school classes. By 1921, with its enrollment swelled by southern newcomers, Wendell Phillips became the city's largest night school. On an average evening, two thousand people attended classes.

Officials in the North, unlike those in the South, urged black children to get an education. "Your job today is to go to school," advised the Board of Education. By 1920, nearly every black child in Chicago between the ages of six and thirteen was in school.

Younger children usually had fewer problems in the northern schools than teenagers. Older students, who had little or no education in the South, were often placed in lower grades. It was not uncommon to find sixteen- and seventeen-year-old boys and girls sitting among the twelve- and thirteen-year-old kids in seventh- and eighth-grade classes.

Students gave the newcomers a chilly reception. African American children born in the North ridiculed the migrants' speech and clothing. The Southerners often responded to such insults with flailing fists. White students at Wendell Phillips

The children's corner at a library. Black children attended the
same schools as white children.
Schomburg Center for Research in Black Culture

controlled social clubs and refused to admit blacks. As the
number of African American students in a school increased,
whites transferred elsewhere. But administrators discouraged
black students from switching to predominantly white schools.

Few blacks taught in Chicago's schools, and white teachers
were woefully ignorant of their black students. Many believed
the young Southerners were retarded or hopelessly backward
and put them in special classes for the "subnormal." One

43

Teenagers in front of a Chicago high school
Library of Congress

instructor believed that "Negro girls in general are slightly retarded because of their early sexual development." Another teacher claimed that "the great physical development of the colored person takes away from the mental development." Even the principal of Wendell Phillips High School believed blacks were only "fitted for special lines of work."

Young African Americans resented being treated as different and inferior. They frequently became problem students or dropouts. Many realized their education would not lead to good jobs. When truant officers confronted them for skipping

44

classes, black children frequently asked, "What work can I get if I go through school?"

As these children understood, black people were severely restricted in the kinds of opportunities available to them, regardless of their education. Paul Robeson, who graduated in the early 1920s from Columbia University Law School, the same school where President Franklin D. Roosevelt received his law degree a few years earlier, never became a practicing lawyer. He knew that a black lawyer, even with a diploma from a prestigious school, had few opportunities for success. Robeson abandoned law and achieved fame as a singer and actor. Other African Americans felt lucky to have careers as railroad porters or post office employees. These jobs were filled by college graduates, high school graduates, and dropouts alike.

Although widespread discrimination in housing, jobs, and schools was a major problem in the 1920s, black people felt a new day was soon coming when there would be much less racial prejudice. This optimism was greatest in the place known as the black mecca, New York's Harlem.

Chapter **6**

Harlem

> In Harlem Negro life is seizing upon its first chances for group expression and self determination. It is—or promises to be—a race capital.
>
> —Alain Locke

On February 17, 1919, the 369th Infantry Regiment paraded in tight formation up New York City's Fifth Avenue. The all-black regiment, nicknamed the Hell-Fighters, had fought for 191 days on the front lines in France. No other American troops had endured as much fighting as these soldiers.

The 369th's white commander, Colonel William Hayward, expressed great pride in these soldiers:

> Well, since July 15, my boys have endured what the French say is the most colossal artillery preparation the Germans have ever made, all kinds of gas, bayonets by the thousand and every other kind of punishment the enemy has in stock. They've stood up under it all, done everything that was demanded of them—a good deal sometimes too—and come through with colors flying and spirits high. I don't believe there are many better soldiers in this war than these Negro boys. I haven't seen any.

The 369th Infantry Regiment fought so heroically that the French government awarded it the Croix de Guerre, one of

A publicity photograph of James Reese Europe and his band
Schomburg Center for Research in Black Culture

that nation's highest tributes. The French also gave the Croix
de Guerre and the Legion of Honor to 171 black officers and
soldiers for their individual bravery.

James Reese Europe, a popular African American band
leader, and his ninety-man military band led the regiment that
cold February day as it paraded uptown to Harlem. Reese,
known as "Big Jim" to his fans, was a showman, and he did not

disappoint the crowd. When the regiment reached 130th Street in Harlem, the band began playing the jazz tune "Here Comes My Daddy." The rows of marching soldiers broke into a jazz step. The delighted throngs of African Americans lining the avenue waved and cheered and rushed into the street to greet the returning troops.

This parade was significant in the hearts and minds of Harlem residents because whites as well as blacks were honoring African American men. These soldiers had helped win "the war to end war." In the minds of many black Americans, it was a turning point in the country's race relations.

An article in the *Messenger,* a black-owned magazine published in New York, expressed the mood of many African Americans. Just as they had fought to make Europe safe for democracy, Negroes would use "physical action in self-defense" and insist on "absolute and unequivocal social equality."

Blacks were more hopeful about their future than at any other time since the end of the Civil War. To Alain Locke, this feeling of confidence and determination represented the "New Negro." And, the Howard University philosophy professor predicted, the New Negro's influence would not be limited to the United States.

African Americans were "the advance guard of the African peoples in their contact with twentieth-century civilization," declared Locke, who had earned a Ph.D. at Harvard University. They had a "sense of mission of rehabilitating the race in world esteem from that loss of prestige for which the fate and conditions of slavery have so largely been responsible. . . . The pulse of the Negro world has begun to beat in Harlem."

Alain Locke
Schomburg Center for
Research in Black Culture

The black population in this section of upper Manhattan had been growing for a dozen years before the Great Migration. At the turn of the century, African Americans, Jews, Poles, Germans, Irish, and Italians all shared the new neighborhood north of 110th Street. Blacks began moving uptown in large numbers after 1900. The modern apartment buildings and wide, tree-lined streets were a welcome change from the crowded neighborhoods downtown.

Several churches, following their congregations, sold their buildings and cemeteries in lower Manhattan for substantial sums and built impressive new buildings in Harlem. One of the oldest was Abyssinian Baptist Church, where Adam Clayton Powell, Sr., was the reverend for many years. It had been founded by slaves just after the Revolutionary War. In the early 1920s, Abyssinian's ten thousand active members moved into a grand new building that had cost $350,000.

Harlem's churches were among the community's wealthiest institutions, and they invested heavily in real estate. In 1911, St. Philip's Episcopal Church, which had recently sold its valuable property on West 25th Street, paid one million dollars for a row of ten new apartment buildings on 135th Street between Lenox and Seventh avenues. It was the largest African American real-estate transaction of the time. The company that negotiated the purchase was Nail & Parker, one of the city's biggest black owned real-estate companies.

Another large firm was the Afro-American Realty Company, owned by Philip A. Payton, Jr. He was called the father of colored Harlem because he encouraged so many blacks to move into the numerous houses and apartment buildings his company owned or managed in the area.

By 1914, about two-thirds of New York's African Americans, some 50,000 people, lived in a twenty-three block area of Harlem. Ten years later, the number had tripled to 150,000. At the same time, over 100,000 white people left Harlem. "They took fright, they became panic stricken, they ran amok," said James Weldon Johnson, a lawyer who had migrated from Florida to Harlem, where he became the first black executive director of the NAACP. "Their conduct could be compared to that of a community in the Middle Ages fleeing before an epidemic of the black plague."

The Great Migration made Harlem the world's largest black metropolis. Harlem "became the symbol of liberty and the Promised Land to Negroes everywhere," exclaimed the Reverend Powell. The migrants came from every southern state along the eastern seaboard: Maryland, Virginia, North

Lenox Avenue was a popular Harlem thoroughfare in the early years of the Great Migration.
Schomburg Center for Research in Black Culture

Marcus Garvey
Schomburg Center for
Research in Black Culture

Carolina, South Carolina, and Florida. They traveled north on trains and on boats. Nearly one-fourth of Harlem's newcomers, however, were not from the South; they were from Jamaica, Trinidad, and other islands in the West Indies.

One of the best-known Jamaican immigrants was Marcus Moziah Garvey, the charismatic leader of the Universal Negro Improvement Association. The UNIA was an organization with an estimated one million members in the United States, the Caribbean, South America, and Africa.

An admirer described Garvey as "a little sawed-off, hammered-down black man with determination written all over his face, and an engaging smile that caught you and compelled you to listen to his story." He was a black nationalist and advocated the creation of a modern Africa governed by native Africans instead of by white European colonists, who main-

W.E.B. DuBois in his office at NAACP headquarters
in New York
Schomburg Center for Research in Black Culture

tained a caste system that kept native blacks in servitude. "Africa for the Africans," Garvey proclaimed.

Other black American leaders, such as Du Bois and Locke, ridiculed the West Indian by calling him the "provisional general of Africa." The UNIA, they joked, stood for "ugliest Negroes in America." Although some disliked Garvey, one writer noted he was "the first Negro in the United States to capture the imagination of the masses."

The UNIA leader's appeal was demonstrated at the first International Convention of the Negro Peoples of the World. The convention, a participant declared, was "the greatest demonstration of colored solidarity in American history." Some twenty-five thousand delegates gathered on September 1, 1920,

53

Chapter 7

The Harlem Renaissance

Harlemites thought the millennium had come. They thought the race problem had at last been solved through art.

—Langston Hughes

On May 2, 1912, three years before the start of the Great Migration, the first all-black concert at Carnegie Hall sold out. It featured Big Jim Europe and his Clef Club, a band of 125 musicians who played banjos, mandolins, guitars, violins, violas, cellos, double basses, drums, and pianos. Besides playing, all of the band members sang. The event, one critic wrote, was "an epoch in the musical life of the Negro." The audience included "many of New York's best white musicians, and also contributors to our Philharmonic and Symphony orchestras."

The popular concert proved, this critic believed, that "the folk song of the Negro has something to give to art—something that is original and convincing because it speaks from the heart." Negro music would be, the writer predicted, "an unexpected force for better understanding between whites and blacks."

As the number of black people in northern cities increased during the Great Migration, they had a growing influence on popular culture. A newspaper article in the early 1920s revealed that the famous composer Irving Berlin "borrowed lilts from the chants of the Negroes of the South." The article continued, "The Harlem dance halls are frequented now by wise stage directors in search of new sensations for something in rehearsal."

Black music and dancing became widely popular in the 1920s, a period dubbed the Jazz Age by novelist F. Scott Fitzgerald. The black composers Eubie Blake and Noble Sissle collaborated on the music for *Shuffle Along.* This 1921 stage show, which popularized a dance called the Charleston, was a big hit at the Sixty-third Street Theatre. Its cast included three people who would become famous actors and singers. Paul Robeson, in his second year at Columbia University Law School, sang bass. By the mid-1920s, he would be appearing in his first movie, *Body and Soul,* a film produced and directed by Oscar Micheaux, a railroad porter turned film maker.

Both Josephine Baker and Florence Mills were in the chorus of *Shuffle Along.* The beautiful Baker moved to Paris, where her exotic cabaret shows gave her a worldwide reputation. Mills went on to become a star in the movies and on stage. She had the leading role in *Dixie to Broadway.* This comedy, the first all-black musical to appear on Broadway, opened at the Broadhurst Theatre in 1924.

The sensational songs and dancing made people curious about the black metropolis above 110th Street. Harlem was suddenly in vogue "as an amusement center," a journalist reported. "Its night life now surpasses that of Broadway itself. From midnight until after dawn it is a seething cauldron of Nubian mirth and hilarity. Never has it been more popular."

Everyone from office workers to Park Avenue socialites, politicians, and European royalty was "doing" Harlem. They went to Jungle Alley along 133rd Street, where the most popular night spots were the Cotton Club and Connie's Inn. At these white-owned establishments, a newspaper account claimed, "one can call the roll of the guests from the Blue Book of Broadway and the Social Register." Harlem's less affluent residents gathered outside to watch people drive up in their Rolls Royces and Deusenbergs.

The clubs featured many performers who soon became widely known. Ethel Waters sang at Leroy's Cafe, and Duke Ellington led the orchestra at the Cotton Club. Other headliners included Fats Waller, Count Basie, Bessie Smith, Louis Armstrong, and Jelly Roll Morton. The Harlem clubs popularized many new dances such as the Texas Tommy, Bunny Hug, Grizzly Bear, Charleston, Black Bottom, Shimmy, Bo-hog, Camel, and Buzzard.

The recording industry, which was just beginning to reach a mass audience, popularized black music. Ethel Waters made her first recording on the Black Swan label, a black-owned recording company. White-owned companies also began to record black music. This competition inspired the Black Swan slogan, "The Only Genuine Colored Record—Others Are Only Passing for Colored."

One of the best-known theaters in Harlem was the Lafayette Theater on Seventh Avenue at 131st Street. Its seats were full most nights for the three-hour show of jazz, vaudeville, dancing girls, and movies. Outside the Lafayette stood the Tree of Hope. This old elm, local lore claimed, would bring jobs to musicians and actors who stood under its branches.

Some of the best entertainment was not held in clubs but in apartments. These were called rent parties, because people charged admission in order to make enough money to pay the rent or other expenses. They were also called shouts, jumps, or struts, which were common southern expressions. For twenty-five cents or so, the parties featured plenty of food, cheap homemade liquor, music, and dancing. One invitation from

Cora Jones, a resident of 187 West 148th Street, read, "Let Your Papa drink the whiskey / Let Your Mama drink the wine / But you come to Cora's and do the Georgia Grind."

On a good night, hundreds of people would come through the door, drop their quarters in a jar, get cups of bathtub gin, and wander through smoky rooms crowded with people from all walks of life. There would be truck drivers and elevator operators, gamblers and prostitutes, Park Avenue socialites and Wall Street investors, gay men and lesbians, writers and artists. Late at night, after they had finished their sets at the clubs, musicians like Duke Ellington or Fats Waller might drop by to play a few songs.

Harlem's most lavish parties were given by A'Lelia Walker, the "Mahogany Millionairess." She was famous, some would say notorious, in the Harlem of the 1920s. A'Lelia was a tall, dark-skinned woman who carried a riding crop and wore a jeweled turban. She owned a mansion created by twin brownstones at 108-110 West 136th Street. The marble entrance to this imposing residence led to gold-colored rooms furnished with expensive Persian carpets and Louis XVI antiques.

People also called A'Lelia the "dekink heiress." This name came from the fact that her mother, Madame C. J. Walker, had invented a popular hair-straightening formula for black women. The straightener and other beauty products earned the former laundress a fortune. When she moved from Indiana to Harlem in 1915, Madame Walker had a manufacturing plant in Indianapolis, a chain of beauty parlors, and fifteen thousand representatives across the nation selling her products. The cosmetics magnate gave money to civil rights organizations, but her daughter enjoyed spending money in other ways.

A'Lelia preferred to hold all-night parties at her apartment nicknamed the "Dark Tower." Guests included princesses,

*A'Lelia Walker was famous
for her parties.*
Schomburg Center for Research
in Black Culture

*Madame C.J. Walker, the richest
black woman in America,
driving her car*
Schomburg Center for Research
in Black Culture

dukes, Wall Street tycoons, actors, railroad porters, and mail-men. A'Lelia's butlers served the whites who had ventured uptown for a taste of exotic Negro life bathtub gin and pigs' feet; her black guests were served champagne and caviar. By the mid-1920s, A'Lelia's guests began to include more black poets, novelists, painters, and sculptors.

Like other prominent African Americans, the cosmetics heiress had decided to work for civil rights by promoting artists. "Civil rights by copyright," some people called it. The idea was popular with many middle-class blacks and intellectuals.

Charles S. Johnson, the sociologist and editor of *Opportunity,* was perhaps the main force behind this movement. It also had support from other people, among them Professor Locke in Washington and Casper Holstein, a native of the Virgin Islands who operated a very profitable gambling ring in Harlem. James Weldon Johnson, an accomplished writer himself, believed that "nothing can go further to destroy race prejudice than the recognition of the Negro as contributor to American civilization."

The Renaissance promoters were not interested in blues or jazz, music they associated with black peasants from the South. They wanted to promote only "high" or traditional culture, such as the Harlem String Quartet and the Harlem Symphony Orchestra. The editors of *Opportunity* searched the nation for promising artists. Locke found sculptor Richmond Barthé in Chicago and urged him to move to New York by promising him financial support from white patrons. And Johnson persuaded Aaron Douglas to give up a job as high school principal in Nebraska and move to New York to paint. Douglas was one of the few black artists to use African themes in his paintings and murals. These two men were among the visual artists who displayed their work in January 1928 at the International House in New York. It was America's first all-Negro art show.

In the arts, the Harlem Renaissance writers are the best remembered. In May of 1925, the publishers of *Opportunity* hosted a dinner to award prizes to poets, novelists, and essayists. The winners that night included Langston Hughes, Claude McKay, Zora Neale Hurston, and Countee Cullen. They were among Harlem's literary stars, whom Hurston irreverently dubbed "Niggerati."

Hughes had grown up in Cleveland, Ohio. As a teenager, he became infatuated with New York's black mecca. "Harlem," he said, "was like a great magnet for the Negro intellectual, pulling him from everywhere." He convinced his father in 1921 to send him to study engineering at Columbia University, which sits on a hill above Harlem. After two semesters, Hughes dropped out of college to devote himself to writing. One of his earliest poems, which he dedicated to Du Bois, was "The Negro Speaks of Rivers." This stirring poem evokes the long history of black people from the great civilization of ancient Egypt to the frontier of the United States.

West Indians, who made up nearly a fourth of Harlem's population, were also prominent in the Renaissance. Claude McKay, a native of Jamaica, came to New York in 1914. McKay became widely known for his poem "If We Must Die," which expressed the Negro's militant mood to fight white violence. "Like men we'll face the murderous, cowardly pack / Pressed to the Wall, dying, but fighting back!" A few years later, his novel *Home to Harlem* became the first book by a black author to reach the bestseller list.

The most prominent woman of the Harlem Renaissance was Zora Neale Hurston. She had been born into a desperately poor family in Jacksonville, Florida. With the help of white

*Claude McKay with
Max Eastman, editor of*
Liberator
Schomburg Center for Research
in Black Culture

friends, the ambitious teenager moved to Baltimore to attend high school. Next, she enrolled in Howard University, where she impressed Professor Locke—who had a reputation for not liking women students.

Hurston left Howard in 1925 for New York City, arriving with only one dollar and fifty cents in her pocket and knowing no one. But Locke had instructed Hurston to see Charles Johnson. He introduced the young woman to a white Fifth

Zora Neale Hurston was one of the few women in the Harlem Renaissance.
Schomburg Center for Research in Black Culture

Avenue matron who gave money to black artists and intellectuals. The recipients of her aid, who included the Howard professor, called the wealthy woman godmother. She helped Hurston get admitted to Barnard, an exclusive women's college across the street from Columbia University. After graduating, Hurston earned a master's degree in anthropology at Columbia. The young anthropologist used her training to study the customs of black people in the South, but she is best remembered for numerous short stories and plays based on the speech, humor, and superstitions of black Southerners.

The best-known Renaissance writer grew up in the North. Countee Cullen had been born in the South, but was raised by adoptive parents in New York City. His adoptive father was the pastor of Little Salem Methodist, one of Harlem's prominent churches. While an undergraduate at New York University, Cullen published his poetry in *Crisis* and *Opportunity*. His poems then appeared in three of the most popular literary magazines of the period, *Harpers'*, *Century,* and *American Mercury*. By the time Cullen received a master's degree from Harvard University, he was being acclaimed as one of the country's best poets. Cullen's famous "The Ballad of the Brown Girl" is a beautiful and simple poem evoking the misery of southern blacks at the mercy of lynch mobs.

White writers, whom Hurston called Negrotarians, also wrote about African American life. The 1920s were an exceptional period for literature in America. Some of the most popular books and plays of the decade were written by whites with black subjects. Eugene O'Neill, whom many people consider to be America's best playwright, wrote several plays with principal black characters, including *Emperor Jones* and *The Hairy Ape*. Paul Robeson starred in both plays.

People up North could demonstrate openly.
Schomburg Center for Research in Black Culture

World War II, Randolph's threat to lead one hundred thousand African Americans on a protest march in Washington forced President Roosevelt to agree to his demand to outlaw discrimination in war industries. Just a few years later, the civil rights leader led the fight that persuaded President Harry Truman to ban racial discrimination in the federal government, which included the military.

Randolph's last great protest occurred in 1963, when he and a coalition of black groups organized the March on Washington. That day, Dr. Martin Luther King, Jr., standing on the steps of the Lincoln Memorial before a crowd of two hundred thousand people, delivered his stirring "I Have a Dream" speech. It was an inspirational high point in the long civil rights movement and helped destroy the South's brutal caste system. The Great Migration was one significant step in that long and continuing struggle to reach the promised land of racial equality.

Endnotes

1 In the Shadow of the Plantation

The best history of black life in a single state during the Great Migration era is Neil R. McMillen's *Dark Journey: Black Mississippians in the Age of Jim Crow* (Urbana: University of Illinois Press, 1989). An enduring account of the development of segregation after the Civil War is C. Vann Woodward's *The Strange Career of Jim Crow* (New York: Oxford University Press, 1974).

A planter's attitudes are expressed in Walker Percy's fascinating autobiography, *Lanterns on the Levee* (New York: Alfred A. Knopf, 1941). Richard Wright's two autobiographical novels, *Black Boy* (New York: Harper and Brothers, 1937) and *American Hunger* (New York: Harper and Brothers, 1937) vividly convey the feelings of a young African American in the segregated South.

Direct quotes are from a variety of primary sources. Southern newspapers such as the New Orleans *Times Picayune,* the Birmingham *News,* the Atlanta *Constitution,* and the Memphis *Commercial Appeal* expressed the views of white Southerners. "Letters of Negro Migrants of 1916–1918," *Journal of Negro History* 4, October 1919, is a valuable collection of letters expressing the dreams and fears of African American migrants.

2 Bound for the Promised Land

James R. Grossman's *Land of Hope: Chicago, Black Southerners, and the Great Migration* (Chicago: University of Chicago Press, 1989) is a very good account of the exodus from the South to Chicago. Another valuable book is Louisa Venable Kennedy's *The Negro Peasant Turns Cityward: Effects of Recent Migrations to*

Northern Centers (New York: Columbia University Press, 1932). The migration was covered extensively in the pages of the black publications the *Chicago Defender* and the *Crisis.*

3   The Black Metropolis

Several good studies have been written about the growth of black communities in northern cities. The best books about Chicago's South Side, in addition to Grossman's *Land of Hope,* are Allan H. Spear's *Black Chicago: The Making of a Negro Ghetto 1890–1920* (Chicago: University of Chicago Press, 1967) and St. Clair Drake and Horace Cayton's *Black Metropolis* (New York: Harcourt, Brace & Company, 1945).

Studies about other cities include Peter Gottlieb's *Making Their Own Way: Southern Blacks' Migration to Pittsburgh, 1916–1930* (Urbana: University of Illinois Press, 1987) and Kenneth L. Kusmer's *A Ghetto Takes Shape: Black Cleveland, 1870–1930* (Urbana: University of Illinois Press, 1976).

Hundreds of letters from migrants to Urban League offices asking for information and assistance are located in the Urban League collection at the Library of Congress. This collection includes Charles S. Johnson's "Chicago Study, Migration Interviews," 1917, which are also good primary sources.

4   Red Summer

The description of the riot of 1919 is based largely on Spear's *Black Chicago.* Charles S. Johnson also compiled an exhaustive report on the 1919 riot for the Chicago Commission on Race Relations.

5   Sticking Together

This chapter is based on information from Spear's *Black Chicago* and Grossman's *Land of Hope.* The paragraph on Negro league baseball is from Michael L. Cooper's *Playing America's Game* (New York: Lodestar, 1993).

6   Harlem

An early study of the development of this well-known black community is Gilbert Osofsky's *Harlem, The Making of a Ghetto* (New York: Harper and Row, 1963). A fascinating photographic essay and collection of reprinted newspaper and magazine articles is *Harlem On My Mind: Cultural Capital of Black America, 1900–1968* (New York: Random House, 1968). The quotes in this chapter are from the *New York Times* and the *New York Herald Tribune* and black publications such as the *Negro World* and the *Amsterdam News*. Clyde Vernon Kiser's *Sea Island to City: A Study of St. Helena Islanders in Harlem and Other Urban Centers* (New York: Columbia University Press, 1932) also contains numerous interviews with recent migrants.

7   The Harlem Renaissance

Good books about the Harlem Renaissance include David Levering Lewis's *When Harlem Was in Vogue* (New York: Oxford University Press, 1981) and Nathan Irvin Huggins's *Harlem Renaissance* (New York: Oxford University Press, 1971).

Biographies, autobiographies, and novels offer valuable insights into the migration and renaissance era: Claude McKay's novel *Home to Harlem* (New York: Harper & Brothers, 1928) and his autobiography, *A Long Way from Home* (New York: Harcourt, Brace & World, 1970); Jervis Anderson's *A. Philip Randolph* (Berkeley: University of California Press, 1972); and David Levering Lewis's *W.E.B. DuBois: Biography of a Race* (New York: Henry Holt and Company, 1993).

Suggested Readings

Hamilton, Virginia. *W.E.B. Dubois* (New York: Crowell, 1972).

———. *Paul Robeson* (New York: Harper & Row, 1974).

Haskins, James S. *Black Music in America: A History Through Its People* (New York: Crowell, 1987).

Lawrence, Jacob. *The Great Migration* (New York: Harper-Collins, 1993).

Lyons, Mary E. *Sorrow's Kitchen: The Life and Folklore of Zora Neale Hurston (New York: Macmillan Children's Book Group, 1990).*

McKissack, Patricia, and Fredrick McKissack. *Madam C.J. Walker: Self-Made Millionaire* (Hillside, NJ: Enslow Publishers, 1992).

Meltzer, Milton. *Langston Hughes* (New York: Crowell, 1968).

Walker, Alice. *Langston Hughes: American Poet* (New York: Crowell, 1974).

Index

Page numbers in *italics* refer to photographs.

About the Author

MICHAEL L. COOPER has been a professional writer for fifteen years. His articles have appeared in various publications, including *Outdoor Life, Travel and Leisure,* and the *Washington Post.* He is the author of four other books for children, most recently *From Slave to Civil War Hero: The Life and Times of Robert Smalls.* He lives in New York City.

DATE DUE

GAYLORD			PRINTED IN U.S.A.